Waterstone's
and The Medical Foundation
Caring for Victims of Torture
celebrate the 50th anniversary
of the Universal Declaration
of Human Rights

Introduced & Illustrated
by Ralph Steadman

An introduction
by Ralph Steadman

Universal Declaration of Human Rights - 50 years - 50 million violations and 50 thoughts...

Without the Universal Declaration of Human Rights my next sentence could contravene some countries' arbitrary rule of law and cause all others to surreptitiously conspire to suppress its blatant defiance of state.

'I have the right to hold an opinion, express it, celebrate it, broadcast it, live by it, and travel with it anywhere I so desire and what's more convince others, by peaceful means, that they should hold that opinion too'.

That in essence is Article 19 of the Universal Declaration of Human Rights and entombed within it is the right of any artist of any faith, impulse or inclination to express him/herself with unbridled passion and conviction sufficient to bestow upon the world a Pandora's box of riches or curses we could probably live without.

Now why was I not told that, or given the little booklet itself back in 1948 when I had just won a scholarship to Abergele Grammar School in North Wales? Javier Perez de Cuellar, the former Secretary General of the United Nations, in an introduction to this little gem states that the UN General Assembly at the time called upon all Member countries to publicise the text of the Declaration and 'to cause it to be disseminated, displayed, read and expounded principally in schools and other educational institutions, without distinction based on the political status of countries of territories'.

Now where was I when these member countries did exactly that? Was I playing truant? Off sick? Drunk?! Not then, not any of that. I was an obedient child of eleven and perfectly capable of digesting the clarity of such proposals, even in the playground.

Were we perhaps off the map? Wales is, after all, only a little country concerned with sheep and Eisteddfods (Welsh Festivals of the Arts). During the war our people had been subjected to a policy of linguistic genocide, the death of the Welsh language. My mother was a loving, law-abiding soul and never spoke Welsh again, at home, 'so as not to be a bother' as she used to say.

Article 19 is obviously a dangerous one amongst twenty nine other equally important human agreements, but it is probably the one article which keeps well hidden within its carefully unbiassed structure the undeniable fact that its content releases the power of the individual to be both artist and maniac. The 1948 United Nations Assembly had unwittingly created a monster, an embarrassing loophole, a well-meaning but desperate humanitarian gesture. In their earnest intentions to neutralise any future tyranny in the shadow of the recent Holocaust freedom of communication was paramount. Slipping it in neatly between 'freedom of thought' (Article 18) and 'freedom of peaceful assembly' (Article 20) should have covered the board but the enemies of democracy are forever busy. Freedom to think is an uncontrollable private act and even peaceful assembly is innocuous as far as it goes - nobody can keep every human being in the whole world in solitary confinement - but broadcasting thought and acting upon it, oh no!

Though Cyberspace may yet find a Noble Destiny, radio and television stations, newspapers, books and printing presses are the first victims of tyranny. They remain the lethal chink of light and therefore of hope against a repressive regime. WEI JING SHENG could be regarded as a lethal chink of light when he was sentenced to 14 years in 1995 for his part in the Tiananmen Square Uprising. The hope that he was still alive was the spur that kept the whole question of Chinese democracy in a state of flux. The difference between Chinese Communism and Chinese culture became apparent to the young. Communism offers no personal freedom. Chinese culture offers a wide spectrum of tradition and evolution and a chance to develop as individuals.

The much maligned philosopher Nietzsche caught the breadth of the world's eternal dilemma in one sentence; 'It is only as an aesthetic phenomenon that existence and the world are permanently justified'.

At the time of its publication every individual of school age should have had the Articles drummed into them like the Ten Commandments which we *did* learn. 'Though shalt not - etc'. The negative was emphasised like public hygiene and what we were not told was no concern of ours. The British Empire was still intact, even then, so everything was assumed to be in order.

The World then still believed that the state knew best and any claim that we might have rights for simply being born was at best a weird piece of human presumption. It sounded like a law for troublemakers, a clarion call to those who think only of revenge. Many crimes are committed in the name of the great cultural revolutions and the icons of their instigation. Neither can the administrators of all repression be free of private thoughts. Who can shave in the morning - or mask their worry lines - without seeing their fear, guilt, and a loathing of their trade? Who does not hear the death knell of those hasty ideologies that twist natural loyalties against their own species and renders them slaves to the cancer that is not enlightenment at all, but the virus that makes them sick and makes them blind.

Within this fatal trap of mid-20th Century political appease-ment, of convenient international diplomacy a tacit agreement was mumbled into a thinks bubble. Pay lip service to the idea of individual human rights but keep pumping the UN Charter which declares that all states have the right to sovereign rule and therefore could, with impunity, conduct their state business like Machiavellian Christians or Muslims or rampant Fundamentalists. They'll go with that. You can't meddle indiscriminately in other people's affairs. It's OK to imprison, torture, maim, murder, rape, disseminate, crush, torment, disinherit, cleanse, help even, behind our blanket blessing, behind our sovereign rights. But the individual? Who he??

The disgust I feel for sovereign rights strengthens my conviction that we have to begin again to establish human rights. We may even have to abandon sovereign rights to protect the individual - you and me - Joe Bloggamovitch and his wife Maria della Francesca, and her sister - and the brother - and the children. Don't forget the children. We see them every night on the telly - desperate, weeping, bleeding, holding out their arms for some evidence of basic human mercy or clutching their meagre belongings as the only thing they can trust. We balefully watch it all as a fact of life, as though they are in another world and we silently count our blessings in our private thoughts, which we are allowed, and then we hastily change the subject.

Expect nothing from the state except your passport and your ticket home to a prison of your country's choice. A free hotel for you and your kind. The rats that came ashore with the cargo have got a sporting chance of survival. They can hide and set up house and they don't need a passport, and they don't speak out except in times of plague.

But you can be an outcast for speaking out, according to the protections sealed into the United Nations Charter which superseded the Treaty of Versailles and the League of Nations resolve after World War 1 (which the US refused to join) requiring member countries to respect territorial independence, while such regimes ruled the world. Hitler used it as his own Bill of Rights. The men in brown shirts, Hombergs and leather overcoats could have you rounded up and killed like a rabid dog, for thinking an original thought. They could call it treason from behind their own wall of sovereign rights and 'Peace in our Time' put the final nail in the coffin of the individual.

I go to bed every night with the private thought that there may come a knock on the door at 3am and it's them, the thought police who chose me tonight.

I think often of Victor JARA, a folk singer and civil rights activist in Chile in the 70s at the time of Allende, who was beaten and had his wrists broken to prevent him from ever stirring people's hearts again. The state paraded him in public to show how strong they were. A sovereign state displayed its power - a eulogy of impotence that instills nothing in an individual's mind but fear and revulsion.

We are all guilty of gross negligence or convenient choice. We have chosen to turn a blind eye to the constant injustice of our own species against our own kind. We no longer deserve to belong to the animal kingdom. We have betrayed an innate sense of survival, the one instinctive law which protects all creatures from extinction. Compassion has been sacrificed on the altar of political expediency.

You may win the battle to be on top for a while but unless the individual is the object of your struggle you will never reach that plateau of certainty to bring you peace of mind. In South Africa they call that state MANDELA. May the whole world reach a state of MANDELA, tomorrow if necessary, but preferably today.

Ralph Steadman 16 August 1998

These are the human rights of

_____

as set forth by the
Universal Declaration of Human Rights

On December 10, 1948 the General Assembly of the United Nations adopted and proclaimed the Universal Declaration of Human Rights the full text of which appears in the following pages. Following this historic act the Assembly called upon all Member countries to publicise the text of the Declaration and "to cause it to be disseminated, displayed, read and expounded principally in schools and other educational institutions, without distinction based on the political status of countries or territories."

Javier Perez de Cuellar
(U.N. SECRETARY GENERAL 1982-1991)

Preamble

Whereas recognition of the inherent dignity and of the equal and inalienable rights of all members of the human family is the foundation of freedom, justice and peace in the world,

Whereas disregard and contempt for human rights have resulted in barbarous acts which have outraged the conscience of mankind, and the advent of a world in which human beings shall enjoy freedom of speech and belief and freedom from fear and want has been proclaimed as the highest aspiration of the common people,

Whereas it is essential, if man is not to be compelled to have recourse, as a last resort, to rebellion against tyranny and oppression, that human rights should be protected by the rule of law,

Whereas it is essential to promote the development of friendly relations between nations,

Whereas the peoples of the United Nations have in the Charter reaffirmed their faith in fundamental human rights, in the dignity and worth of the human person and in the equal rights of men and women and have determined to promote social progress and better standards of life in larger freedom,

Whereas Member States have pledged themselves to achieve, in co-operation with the United Nations, the promotion of universal respect for and observance of human rights and fundamental freedoms,

Whereas a common understanding of these rights and freedoms is of the greatest importance for the full realisation of this pledge,

Now, Therefore

The General Assembly

proclaims

This Universal Declaration of Human Rights

as a common standard of achievement for all peoples and all nations, to the end that every individual and every organ of society, keeping this Declaration constantly in mind, shall strive by teaching and education to promote respect for these rights and freedoms and by progressive measures, national and international, to secure their universal and effective recognition and observance, both among the peoples of Member States themselves and among the peoples of territories under their jurisdiction.

Article 1.

All human beings are born free and equal in dignity and rights. They are endowed with reason and conscience and should act towards one another in a spirit of brotherhood.

Article 2.

Everyone is entitled to all the rights and freedoms set forth in this Declaration, without distinction of any kind, such as race, colour, sex, language, religion, political or other opinion, national or social origin, property, birth or other status. Furthermore, no distinction shall be made on the basis of the political, jurisdictional or international status of the country or territory to which a person belongs, whether it be independent, trust, non-self-governing or under any other limitation of sovereignty.

Article 3.

Everyone has the right to life, liberty and security of person.

Article 4.

No one shall be held in slavery or servitude; slavery and the slave trade shall be prohibited in all their forms.

Article 5.

No one shall be subjected to torture or to cruel, inhuman or degrading treatment or punishment.

Article 6.

Everyone has the right to recognition everywhere as a person before the law.

Article 7.

All are equal before the law and are entitled without any discrimination to equal protection of the law. All are entitled to equal protection against any discrimination in violation of this Declaration and against any incitement to such discrimination.

Article 8.

Everyone has the right to an effective remedy by the competent national tribunals for acts violating the fundamental rights granted him by the constitution or by law.

Article 9.

No one shall be subjected to arbitrary arrest, detention or exile.

Article 10.

Everyone is entitled in full equality to a fair and public hearing by an independent and impartial tribunal, in the determination of his rights and obligations and of any criminal charge against him.

Article 11.

(1) Everyone charged with a penal offense has the right to be presumed innocent until proved guilty according to law in a public trial at which he has had all the guarantees necessary for his defence.

(2) No one shall be held guilty of any penal offense on account of any act or omission which did not constitute a penal offense, under national or international law, at the time when it was committed. Nor shall a heavier penalty be imposed than the one that was applicable at the time the penal offense was committed.

Article 12.

No one shall be subjected to arbitrary interference with his privacy, family, home or correspondence, nor to attacks upon his honour and reputation. Everyone has the right to the protection of the law against such interference or attacks.

Article 13.

(1) Everyone has the right to freedom of movement and residence within the borders of each state.

(2) Everyone has the right to leave any country, including his own, and to return to his country.

Article 14.

(1) Everyone has the right to seek and to enjoy in other countries asylum from persecution.

(2) This right may not be invoked in the case of prosecutions genuinely arising from non-political crimes or from acts contrary to the purposes and principles of the United Nations.

Article 15.

(1) Everyone has the right to a nationality.

(2) No one shall be arbitrarily deprived of his nationality nor denied the right to change his nationality.

Article 16.

(1) Men and women of full age, without any limitation due to race, nationality or religion, have the right to marry and to found a family. They are entitled to equal rights as to marriage, during marriage and at its dissolution.

(2) Marriage shall be entered into only with the free and full consent of the intending spouses.

(3) The family is the natural and fundamental group unit of society and is entitled to protection by society and the State.

Article 17.

(1) Everyone has the right to own property alone as well as in association with others.

(2) No one shall be arbitrarily deprived of his property.

Article 18.

Everyone has the right to freedom of thought, conscience and religion; this right includes freedom to change his religion or belief, and freedom, either alone or in community with others and in public or private, to manifest his religion or belief in teaching, practice, worship and observance.

Article 19.

Everyone has the right to freedom of opinion and expression; this right includes freedom to hold opinions without interference and to seek, receive and impart information and ideas through any media and regardless of frontiers.

Article 20.

(1) Everyone has the right to freedom of peaceful assembly and association.

(2) No one may be compelled to belong to an association.

Article 21.

(1) Everyone has the right to take part in the government of his country, directly or through freely chosen representatives.

(2) Everyone has the right of equal access to public service in his country.

(3) The will of the people shall be the basis of the authority of government; this will shall be expressed in periodic and genuine elections which shall be by universal and equal suffrage and shall be held by secret vote or by equivalent free voting procedures.

Article 22.

Everyone, as a member of society, has the right to social security and is entitled to realisation, through national effort and international co-operation and in accordance with the organisation and resources of each State, of the economic, social and cultural rights indispensable for his dignity and the free development of his personality.

Article 23.

(1) Everyone has the right to work, to free choice of employment, to just and favourable conditions of work and to protection against unemployment.

(2) Everyone, without any discrimination, has the right to equal pay for equal work.

(3) Everyone who works has the right to just and favourable remuneration ensuring for himself and his family an existence worthy of human dignity, and supplemented, if necessary, by other means of social protection.

(4) Everyone has the right to form and to join trade unions for the protection of his interests.

Article 24.

Everyone has the right to rest and leisure, including reasonable limitation of working hours and periodic holidays with pay.

Article 25.

(1) Everyone has the right to a standard of living adequate for the health and well-being of himself and of his family, including food, clothing, housing and medical care and necessary social services, and the right to security in the event of unemployment, sickness, disability, widowhood, old age or other lack of livelihood in circumstances beyond his control.

MOTHER and CHILD Christmas 1983
Ralph STEAD

(2) Motherhood and childhood are entitled to special care and assistance. All children, whether born in or out of wedlock, shall enjoy the same social protection.

Article 26.

(1) Everyone has the right to education. Education shall be free, at least in the elementary and fundamental stages. Elementary education shall be compulsory. Technical and professional education shall be made generally available and higher education shall be equally accessible to all on the basis of merit.

(2) Education shall be directed to the full development of the human personality and to the strengthening of respect for human rights and fundamental freedoms. It shall promote understanding, tolerance and friendship among all nations, racial or religious groups, and shall further the activities of the United Nations for the maintenance of peace.

(3) Parents have a prior right to choose the kind of education that shall be given to their children.

Article 27.

(1) Everyone has the right freely to participate in the cultural life of the community, to enjoy the arts and to share in scientific advancement and its benefits.

(2) Everyone has the right to the protection of the moral and material interests resulting from any scientific, literary or artistic production of which he is the author.

Article 28.

Everyone is entitled to a social and international order in which the rights and freedoms set forth in this Declaration can be fully realised.

Article 29.

(1) Everyone has duties to the community in which alone the free and full development of his personality is possible.

(2) In the exercise of his rights and freedoms, everyone shall be subject only to such limitations as are determined by law solely for the purpose of securing due recognition and respect for the rights and freedoms of others and of meeting the just requirements of morality, public order and the general welfare in a democratic society.

(3) These rights and freedoms may in no case be exercised contrary to the purposes and principles of the United Nations.

Article 30.

Nothing in this Declaration may be interpreted as implying for any State, group or person any right to engage in any activity or to perform any act aimed at the destruction of any of the rights and freedoms set forth herein.

**Introduced & Illustrated
by Ralph Steadman**

Designed by
Interbrand Newell and Sorrell